THE INVITATION

IAIN H. MURRAY

THE BANNER OF TRUTH TRUST

THE BANNER OF TRUTH TRUST
3 Murrayfield Road, Edinburgh EH12 6EL
P.O. BOX 621, *Carlisle, Pennsylvania* 17013, *U.S.A.*

*

©Banner of Truth 1967
First published 1967
Reprinted 1973
Reprinted 1984
Reprinted 1988
Reprinted 1998
ISBN 0 85151 171 6

*

Printed in Great Britain by
Polton Press, Edinburgh

The Necessity for Discussion

An invariable characteristic of true preaching has been the assurance that the proclamation of the gospel is the divinely ordained means for the conviction and conversion of sinners. 'It pleased God by the foolishness of preaching to save them that believe' (1 Cor. 1: 21), and in accordance with this persuasion evangelicals have never been content to preach the Word without seeing any change wrought in their hearers. Of the sermons of some men it has been said,

They may be correctly cold and correctly dull!
Faultily faultless, icily regular, spendidly null . .

but the man who has a scriptural view of the pulpit and of the gospel will desire to preach like Richard Baxter 'as an express from another world', or like M'Cheyne who, as one of his hearers said, 'preached as if he was dyin' a'most to have ye converted'.

Wherever preaching has ceased to require an individual response and wherever hearers are left with the impression that there is no divine command requiring their repentance and faith, true Christianity has withered away. The presentation of Christianity as a rehearsal of facts, without any attempt to apply these facts to the conscience, and without any call to trust in Jesus as a mighty Saviour, falls far short of apostolic preaching. When two London evangelical ministers of a former generation, Matthew Wilks and John Hyatt, took their leave of each other as Hyatt lay dying, Wilks asked, 'Well, John, could you trust your soul in the hands of Jesus Christ now?' 'Yes,' came the fervent reply, 'a million! a million souls!' This is the persuasion which is essential to gospel preaching.

[1]

In the following pages, then, there is no discussion about whether it is right to invite men to come to Christ. That issue should be indisputable to those who believe Scripture. Nor is it an open question whether man's responsibility to repent and believe should be emphasized in evangelism. As we have already said, without such an emphasis there can be no evangelism at all in any biblical sense of the word. Our discussion concerns a different issue, namely, whether it is in the best interests of evangelism to distinguish between hearers at the close of a sermon by inviting those who wish to receive Christ to come to the front. If the invitation system, as this practice may be called, can be shown to rest upon what the Scriptures say about coming to Christ, or upon what may be legitimately deduced from the doctrine of man's responsibility, then it may be justly claimed that to oppose the system is to oppose Scripture. But until this is shown it cannot be fairly implied that those who do not give 'the invitation' are less concerned with evangelism than those who do. The question as to whether the practice stands on a scriptural basis must be settled first. We cannot be more evangelical than the New Testament.

It is probable, however, that some of those who advocate the invitation system, would not claim specific scriptural warrant for the practice. They would be content to say that it is a useful and successful method in the fulfilment of a scriptural objective – the bringing of individuals to a personal decision. And, it might well be added, because this is simply a question of *method*, is it worthwhile debating and arguing about it? To the latter question we reply that the practice itself *compels* debate and that for at least two reasons.

First, although, for more than a hundred years, evangelism in Britain has sometimes been accompanied by the use of 'after-meetings', or of cards which individuals are to sign as an affirmation of faith, the practice of summoning people to the front as the natural climax of a gospel message and as an integral part of an evangelistic service has been comparatively rare. But the prominence given to 'the invitation' in the crusades of recent years, coupled with earnest appeals from

[2]

evangelists that ministers should use the same method, is now forcing all evangelical congregations to examine their former omission. If, as it is represented, the appeal to come forward is the 'climax' of an evangelistic sermon, can churches which are evangelical be satisfied to remain without the practice? And this question is all the more pointed when the numerical success attending the use of 'the invitation' is compared with the small response attending much preaching today. In the contemporary conditions of spiritual need, the testimony which well-known leaders are giving to the value of 'the invitation' is bound to cause discussion amongst those who are concerned about these conditions. For desiring further discussion before accepting a practice which is not part of the evangelical tradition of this land Christians should not be blamed. Though for some evangelicals the pragmatic argument for an immediate general adoption of the invitation system (namely, the numerical results which have attended its use in the modern crusades) may appear irresistible, there are others who think that a closer, scriptural examination of the innovation is necessary before it is received. 'Let every man be fully persuaded in his own mind.'

Secondly, as Leighton Ford, one of the latest exponents of the invitation system, reminds us, it is essential in using 'the invitation' that the evangelist should give straightforward directions which are clearly understood. All vagueness is to be avoided: 'The invitation should not be, "If there is anyone here who might want to come, you could come, or you could wait and see me afterward." Let it rather be: "God is calling, Come now. Come here".'[1] Yet despite the publicity which has been given in recent years we think it may be fairly questioned, whether even now it is clear just *what* is being required of those who come forward. Is the walk forward an outward declaration of an inner saving decision already made by the hearer in the seat, just an 'act of witness'? Why then are they told to 'come forward to *receive* Christ'? How is 'receiving Christ' related to coming forward? Is there any relation? The most popular description of 'the invitation' as an 'act of commitment to Christ', leaves these questions quite unresolved,

[3]

and unless the system is to shelter behind the vagueness which it professes to avoid, there are certain very fundamental considerations which must be clarified.

Before writing the following pages I sought to understand the case which is put forward for 'the invitation', both by reading what its advocates have to say and by attending meetings where a public appeal was made for decisions. I do not want to mis-state that case. This leads, however, to a difficulty. To shroud in anonymity the quotations which I shall give would be both irritating to the reader and against the interests of a fair debate. Discussion of a controversial subject demands documented references. On the other hand, the danger is that, once names are quoted, interest is switched from the clarification of ideas to the person whose words are under review. Were it possible to present the arguments for the invitation system in the words of men no longer living, this danger might, in measure, be avoided, but we know of no former evangelical preacher on record who has used 'the invitation' in precisely the way it is being used today. While statements from Finney or Moody might be interesting in this connection, they could not be taken as the most cogent reasons for the modern use of the system. I have therefore concluded that the only way adequately to present the arguments used to support the practice is to quote directly from the most forceful contemporary spokesman for gospel preaching who uses it, namely, Dr Billy Graham. I can only hope that the reader will prefer this to a veiled and oblique criticism of a position which the American evangelist is well known to hold, and that it will be borne in mind that what is under consideration is not a question of personalities.

During the 'Greater London Crusade' in 1966, each meeting included a public 'invitation' and a brief explanation why it was being given. The design of 'the invitation' was professedly simple. Little knowledge and no emotion, the hearers were told, is needed to respond: it is 'an act of commitment to Christ', expressed by leaving one's seat and assembling with others in front of the preacher's platform. The urgency for people to make such a move forward is not conveyed by the working up of any excitement in the meeting but by the reasons which the preacher gives to prompt a response on the part of the unconverted. To a greater or lesser extent the sermon has already shown the need of a change in those who do not know Christ, and the importance of 'the invitation' is that it is represented as providing the opportunity for such a change to take place. The hearer is told that his need is to 'let Christ come into his heart', which is explained as meaning '(1) repent, (2) receive Him by faith', to which Graham adds such words as these: 'This is how we are going to do it – Get up right now and come to the front.'[2] Curtis Mitchell, author of *Those Who Came Forward*, says the words Graham uses in making the appeal vary little and he gives us the following typical example:

'I am going to ask you to come forward. Up there – down there – I want you to come. You come right now – quickly. If you are with friends or relatives, they will wait for you.

'Don't let distance keep you from Christ. It's a long way, but Christ went all the way to the Cross because He loved you. Certainly you can come these few steps and give your life to Him . . .'[3]

To those who hesitate, Graham may add: 'God is speaking to you. Get up and come right now . . . a little voice says, "You ought to come to Christ". Come now quickly! You may never have another moment. You have to come by faith. You need Christ, you get up and come . . .' In all this there is no pressure beyond a solemn insistence on the one fact that those who want to receive Christ must come to the front.

When after moments of silence many are gathered in front of the platform, the spiritual implications of what is being done are again emphasized. Addressing those who have responded to the invitation, Graham says, 'You have come tonight to Jesus Christ, you have come to receive Him into your heart', or 'Give your life to God. You do it now!' And in the hope that those he is now addressing have just done this, Graham assures them: 'He receives you; He died for you; He says, "Thy sins are forgiven." You accept that. The past is forgiven, God forgets . . . He cannot even see your sins.

[5]

Accept by faith that He comes into your heart.' Then follows a prayer which those standing at the front are asked to repeat aloud after the preacher: 'O God, I am a sinner. I am sorry for my sin. I am willing to turn from my sin. I receive Christ as Saviour. I confess Him as Lord. From this moment on I want to follow Him and serve Him in the fellowship of His Church.' Before those who have come forward move out of the service to be counselled, Graham finally gives them some practical advice such as, 'Read the Bible . . . Pray . . . Witness . . . Get into the Church to worship God,' and in these words the spiritual change in those who have responded is again assumed, 'You are going to be tempted, but you are His child, get up again . . .'

We turn now to examine the reasons which are given to prove the correctness of giving this 'invitation' at the end of an address. Graham repeatedly gave two major reasons to his hearers at Earl's Court, and there is a third. These are:

1. Christ always called people publicly and this statement is confirmed by texts such as 'Follow me', or 'Whosoever shall confess me before men, him will I confess before my Father which is in heaven.'

2. 'Coming out,' it is said, 'settles it and seals it.' We did not hear this elaborated but the implied meaning seems to be that a step made publicly is more likely to be decisive and irrevocable.'There's something about coming forward and standing here. It's an outward expression of an inward decision.'[4]

3. According to John Pollock's authorized biography of Graham, the invitation has value as a visual demonstration to the uncommitted. Pollock gives a quotation to the effect that a televised crusade meeting with its invitation and response seen by thousands is more valuable than Graham merely televised from a studio: 'When the average, moral, reputable American sees Dr. Graham in a studio telling him he needs to be "born again", his first impulse will be to discredit him as a religious fanatic. But if the viewer sees thousands of respectable, normal people listening and consenting to all this he hears, and then *sees* hundreds voluntarily get up and walk to the front in

response to a low pressure request, he'll begin to consider the message and situation with some sincere, honest interest. It's much easier to say a single speaker is wrong than to discredit the conviction and decision of thousands.'[5]

The Invitation and Scripture

Of the three reasons given above only the first claims direct scriptural support. We have therefore, in the first place, to consider whether the texts quoted above are decisive either for or against the practice now being discussed? The command of Jesus, 'Follow me', to his future apostles and to others in the days of His flesh, is alleged to justify the calling out of people to the front because Jesus demanded an outward identification with Himself on the part of those who would be His disciples. But what does 'Follow me' or 'Come unto me' mean from the lips of the Son of God? Are these primarily directions which require a physical and local movement? That it might some-times include the local aspect (like Zacchæus' descent from the tree) is clear enough from the gospel narratives, but even in the days of Christ's visible presence a spiritual identification with Him by repentance and faith was clearly the fundamental sense of the words, and once He was no longer physically present *there could be no other sense*. No man can now come to Jesus with his feet, and even when He was upon earth, a coming to Him in that way never accomplished what it is now implied may be accomplished by those who walk to the front. There is no parallel between the modern appeal and the Lord's words, nevertheless the appeal is given as though Christ Himself endorses the evangelist's call to 'get up quickly'. 'He went to the cross to die, bleeding for you; you can come a few steps in this beautiful arena for Him'. 'Come now, if you do not receive Him you will die in your sins, come forward. . . .' And con-sequently those who do assemble at the front are treated as those responding to *Christ's command*. Mitchell reports the following typical conversation between Charles Riggs (the director of all the counselling in the 1966 Greater London Crusade) and an enquirer:

' "You've come forward to receive Christ. How do you know this is what you must do?"

"Well, it says so in the Bible."

"Then God is saying it, isn't He?"

"Yes, I guess He is."

"And there's no higher authority than God, is there?"

"No, of course not."

"Then you accept the Word of God, don't you?" '

When the answer to the last question 'is in the affirmative', Mitchell continues, 'as is generally the case, Riggs puts it all in a capsule for the novice – "Think of it like this," he says, "God says it. On faith, you believe it. And that settles it." '[6]

As we shall seek to elaborate later, all this reasoning proceeds on the assumption that coming to the front is tantamount to, if not identical with coming to Christ, and it is only where such a confusion of thought exists that a text like 'Follow me' can be quoted as a proof of the rightness of the practice.

We turn then to the second text which, it is alleged, proves the public 'invitation' to be in harmony with Christ's command, 'Whosoever shall confess me before men . . .' (Matt. 10: 32). The point to be settled over this verse is straightforward: Is Christ here saying that by an *act* of confession we *become* Christians or is He teaching that one indispensable mark of those who *are* Christians is that they live a life which openly acknowledges Him? Is not the modern evangelistic call to confess Christ by coming to the front, in order to receive Him by faith, a reversal of the New Testament order? To confess Christ is the spiritual duty of a Christian. It is no part of the gospel to say that compliance with certain outward duties will help us to *become* Christians. Yet the whole invitation system inevitably gives the impression that 'confessing Christ' by moving forward is in order to conversion. Graham is quite specific about the fact that the confession which is required in 'the invitation' to walk forward or stand up is for those who until that moment have been non-Christians. J. C. Pollock records how, preaching in Berlin in 1954, Graham, having

[8]

reached the end of his address, 'cried: "Those who want to *decide for* Christ, stand up," the interpreter used words that to the German implied "Do you want to *confess* Christ?" Tens of thousands stood: every deacon, every pastor: every layman who believed himself a disciple. Billy said, "No, no, you misunderstand". He explained again the meaning of repentance, faith, a first-time decision for Christ, the new birth. John Bolton is "absolutely sure" that the audience understood the second translation. Some sat, large numbers stood.'[7]

If this confessing of Christ by response to an appeal is not for Christians it is impossible to see how Matthew 10: 32 can be used to support the practice. It can only be done by interpreting the confession (which Jesus promises to reward) in a way which the analogy of Scripture does not allow. If this text were, in fact, a guide to the way sinners are to make a 'decision for Christ', it would mean a radically new interpretation of scores of texts in the New Testament, texts which evangelical Christians have always understood to give the distinguishing characteristics of those who are truly born again, not *the way* in which that rebirth takes place. For example, John 8: 31 does not teach that remaining faithful to Christ's Word *makes* us true disciples, nor does John 15: 8 say that fruit-bearing is the process by which we become true Christians, though these texts (and many others) could be violated to give them such a sense. The distinction we are making here is simply the old Protestant distinction which preached works as a necessary evidence of salvation, not as the prior condition of salvation.

In this discussion it is not, of course, in dispute whether an initial act of confessing Christ was required by the apostles from those who, receiving the gospel, were consequently admitted into the fellowship of the Church. Such a confession was included in baptism. But before anyone concludes that 'the invitation' merely changes the mode in which the confession is made, it has to be asserted that baptism never had the place in evangelism which the invitation system has now. The place of the ordinance in the missionary outreach of the Church is to seal those who have professed Christ as a result of teaching (Matt. 28: 19), and before that confession could be made (in a way which thereafter publicly identified converts with the churches and with Christ) office-bearers, entrusted with the discipline of the Church, had to be satisfied that the persons made a credible profession and were instructed in the faith. From some examples in the Acts it may be argued that this satisfaction may be obtained in a very brief time. But the experience of the churches after their initial formation by the apostles, proved otherwise; hence arose that class of person called 'catechumens', and later in Church history, 'the awakened', who were not immediately received into the full membership of the churches by public profession as soon as they indicated an interest in the gospel.

General biblical principles (such as, 'Lay hands suddenly on no man'), confirmed by the long record of Church history, show that the sudden public profession of Christ by persons whose experience has been tested neither by time nor by the examination of pastors, is calculated to be disastrous. For this very reason we know of no evangelical minister who would at once baptize people who 'responded' at the end of a service.

Baptism and coming to the front are two essentially different things. One is an act which confirms the promises of salvation to believers, the other is a device intended to help men *become* believers. One bears witness to salvation, the other is represented as actually accomplishing something towards our salvation. One is an action commanded by Christ, the other is not.

C. G. Finney (1792–1875), apparently the first professed evangelist to call people forward during a service to a position which he called 'the anxious seat', defended the practice on the grounds that it answered the purpose which baptism had in the days of the apostles. Professor Dod of Princeton commented on this argument: 'Though he supposes that the anxious seat occupies "the precise place" that baptism did, we can by no means consent to receive it as an equivalent. Baptism was, indeed, a test of character, since obedience or disobedience was exercised in view of a divine command; but the anxious seat cannot operate thus, except by arrogating to itself a similar authority.'[8]

[10]

Before leaving this examination of the alleged scriptural evidence for the invitation system we may note a certain inconsistency amongst those who approve of the practice. For example, Harold J. Ockenga, of Boston, speaking at the World Congress on Evangelism (convened in Berlin under the chairmanship of Billy Graham, Autumn, 1966), judged that it was valid to use or not to use 'the invitation' because conversions occur in both instances: 'We must conclude that we cannot be exclusive in our methodology, nor can we sit in judgment upon those who use a different methodology in evangelism from our own.'[9] Ockenga appears to argue that both the use and the non-use of 'the invitation' are right, as God blesses both ministries. But if the evangelist's choice in employing 'the invitation' is an optional one it cannot have scriptural evidence to warrant it, for in that case the evangelical preacher would be under an obligation and have no option. If there *is* biblical authority for the practice, the non-user is failing in duty even though God may bless his ministry in spite of its deficiency. On the other hand, if there is *no* biblical authority, the argument that 'Jesus always called people publicly' must be dropped.

The measure of uncertainty in those who use the invitation system over the scriptural evidence is perhaps not unrelated to the importance they give to subsidiary arguments and to these we now turn.

The Psychological Argument

The second argument used to support the invitation is expressed by the words: 'There is something about coming forward which settles it.' This is evidently an appeal to what is regarded as a sound interpretation of the human personality. The unwillingness of the unconverted is regarded as the basic spiritual problem: this problem the Spirit meets by conviction of sin. When this occurs the individual experiences misery, 'and this misery brings about pressure on his will to do something about it'. At this point the evangelist must strike in with an invitation which provides, Graham believes, the right emotional outlet for those in this troubled condition. Defend-

[11]

ing the practice, he argues: 'Many psychologists would say it is psychologically sound. One of the reasons why our films and television dramas usually have a bad effect is because they stir the emotion to a high pitch and do not offer any practical outlet for action.'[10]

In one of the latest books to support the invitation system, *The Christian Persuader*, Leighton Ford puts the same argument more fully: 'I am convinced that the giving of some kind of public invitation to come to Christ is not only theologically correct, but also emotionally sound. Men need this opportunity for expression. The inner decision for Christ is like driving a nail through a board. The open declaration of it is like clinching the nail on the other side, so that it is not easily pulled out. Impression without expression can lead to depression. Prof. William James[11] said, "When once the judgment is decided let a man commit himself; let him lay on himself the necessity of doing more, let him lay on himself the necessity of doing all. Let him take a public pledge if the case allows. Let him envelop his resolution with all the aids possible." '[12]

These quotations summarize the psychological case for 'the invitation'. Regarding the consent of man's will as the main objective to be gained, it is supposed that a response which involves action before others will commit people's wills more surely than if they were left individually to seek Christ in private. Thus Ford, linking the alleged biblical argument with the psychological, represents the advantage of the appeal to come forward 'as a means of obeying Christ's command to confess Him before men, and a step which will help to make the decision definite and clear-cut'. Such is the weakness of the will, and so closely (it is presumed) are the operations of the Spirit to be identified with the actual procedures of the meeting, that to fail to give 'the invitation' at the decisive moment is to risk a cessation of the 'pressure' and consequently the possible loss of souls who may relapse into their former state of unwillingness. The great need, then, is for the will to be immediately and openly *committed*, and the more public the action the less likely is a relapse. Presumably it is for this reason that, even when the place in which a meeting is held makes coming to the front inconvenient, the invitation system favours the raising of the hand or the waving of a handkerchief in preference to no public action at all.

This reasoning, which was first clearly related to evangelism by the cool intellect of Charles G. Finney in the 1830's, claims to be psychologically sound. It seems to be more or less what Graham means by a *public* response 'settling it' for the individual. The following incident may illustrate the point. A few years ago Graham was preaching in London on a Sunday night. The end of his sermon at 8.30 p.m. was immediately followed by a broadcast half-hour of hymn singing so that he was not able to give the invitation till the broadcast ended. The response was then disappointing and Graham found the explanation for this in the fact that the call did not at once follow the sermon. In other words 'the pressure' was off after thirty minutes had elapsed and the effect of the appeal was consequently diminished.

It has not, however, escaped the notice of some who are also interested in psychology, but who do not claim to be evangelicals, that the very fact that the invitation system harmonizes with certain features in our psychological make-up leaves it open to serious objections. These critics argue that the way conversions are produced under this system by a pressure on the will is little different from the way in which 'conversions' which make no claim to be Christian at all often take place. The 'conditioning' of a large crowd of people in a controlled environment, with methods of persuasive suggestion leading to a demand for a public response – an emotional release – is psychologically certain, they say, to provide results regardless of whether the crowd meets in the name of religion, entertainment or politics. Modern psychiatrists like William Sargant have analysed some of the physiological processes which make this the case, and crusade opponents like George Target have, on these grounds, subjected the invitation system to an uncomfortable scrutiny: 'All present are told to pray, instructed to close their eyes and bow the head, and the form of words is the auto-suggestive one that hundreds of others are

[13]

already going forward, finding happiness, peace, love, God . . .
The counsellors planted all over the audience make the first few
moves, create the sense that the statement is true even when it
very often is not . . . it might all be true, there might be some
nameless peace down there with all the others . . . the tension
screws to breaking point and beyond . . . The wonder is that
so few actually obey.'[13]

The Billy Graham Organization has repeatedly disavowed in
recent years the presence of any emotional element in the meetings, influencing the will to act when the appeal is given, and it
is often pointed out that the hymn, 'Just as I am . . . I come,'
which used to be sung while the invitation was being given, is
no longer used. But this ignores the fact that the main pressure
on people to come forward was, and is, the idea constantly
conveyed by the preacher that the step forward is of great
spiritual importance. Linked with this is the clear implication
that a failure to respond in the manner required is a deliberate
refusal to obey God. This alone is enough to account for
tension. Says Mitchell, Graham's friend, with regard to the
invitation: 'His plea may be soft spoken but it is packed
suddenly with an electric urgency.' The hymn may have been
dropped but the teaching that those who get up are *coming to
Jesus* still underlies the whole invitation.

We did not quote Target because we think that his
psychology is sound when it comes to understanding the
supernatural ways of God in bringing dead sinners to life, but
we believe that because Graham's thinking is also defective at
this point, his practice is open to charges which could not be
made if he kept more closely to biblical evangelism. Yet not
only does Graham not meet these charges satisfactorily, he
seems unaware of the danger there is in attempting to justify
the invitation, or conversion itself, by appeals to psychology.
In a sermon on conversion which is printed in *Those Who
Come Forward*, the evangelist appeals to the testimony of
psychologists to show man's need of conversion:

'A Chicago psychologist once said, "This generation needs
converting more than any generation in history".

'A famous British psychologist recently said, "We are so

psychologically constituted as to need converting, and if the church fails to convert people, we psychologists are going to have to do it." So even psychology is recognizing the need for man to be converted.

'The Bible teaches that you must be converted to enter Heaven. The psychiatrist teaches that you must be converted in order to get the most out of life.'[14]

These might be passed over as somewhat unguarded statements, but what are we to say of the following explanation of the appeal to go forward at the close of a sermon? It is given by the author of the above book, who is described by Graham in its Preface as being in a unique position to observe his work:

'Wherever he is, if a man goes forward, either in fact or in spirit, the result is a change.'[15]

'What takes place?' Psychologists, psychiatrists, theologians and evangelists have all tried to explain.

'Gordon Allport, noted psychologist, says: "A man's religion is the audacious bid he makes to bind himself to creation and the Creator. It is his ultimate attempt to enlarge and complete his personality by finding the supreme context in which he rightly belongs."

'Then perhaps conversion is the ultimate spiritual step towards that end.'[16]

We hope enough has been said to show that a defence of 'the invitation' in the name of psychology is a perilous procedure which may ultimately lead to the discrediting of true evangelical experience altogether. When it comes to the things of God modern psychology is a broken reed, but if, instead of recognizing it as such, we treat it as an authority there will be a nemesis ahead for evangelicalism. Biblical practices do not need the endorsement of modern psychology. And while we need to defend the truth before an unbelieving world, it is no part of our commission to justify practices which are not biblical by the precarious method of an appeal to the opinion of psychologists.

The truth is that under all preaching, and especially where there are large crowds, there will be results which can be explained on a purely naturalistic basis. David Hume, the 18th-century philosopher who scorned the gospel, noted a colourful instance of this when he was present in an immense open-air gathering where George Whitefield was preaching. So vast was the crowd that those on the circumference were quite beyond earshot of the preacher. Yet Hume says that as he wandered on the outskirts of the congregation he was amazed at the evidences of emotion which met him at every step. 'He paused at length by the side of a woman who was weeping piteously, and inquired, "My good woman, what are you crying for?" – "O sir! for the parson's sermon." – "But can you hear what the parson is saying?" – "No, sir." – "Have you heard anything since he began?" – "No, sir." – "Pray tell me, then, what for do you cry?" – "O sir! don't you see that holy wag of his head?" '[17] Hume's jeer has a point. Some people can be conditioned by a large crowd. No doubt if 18th century gospel preachers had given an 'appeal' they would have had many like this woman coming forward. When they choose rather to leave the credit of their ministry and the gospel to changed lives and characters, they cut away the grounds of criticism which a public appeal would have given Hume (the predecessor of many modern psychologists) had he observed individuals such as this woman going to the front. And they also spared themselves the unedifying necessity of having to demonstrate how many of those who thus publicly 'accepted Christ' endured.

It is certainly possible to argue that 'the psychological argument', far from supporting the validity of the invitation system, exposes further reasons for calling it into question. Worldly wisdom, whether in the form of philosophy or psychology, will never ultimately be found to be an ally of the gospel.

The Invitation as a Visual Demonstration

The third argument for the invitation system, given in Pollock's authorized biography of Graham, might be passed over, for it is not a formal reason given by the evangelist himself why hearers should come forward. The argument is that the approach of hundreds or thousands to the front is a visual

[16]

demonstration to the remainder who are uncommitted, confirming the truth which has been preached. Yet while Graham may not announce that he wants 'the invitation' to have this effect, both the crusade policy[18] and his spoken words are directed to that end. 'There are many people coming to Christ in Earl's Court tonight, coming down every aisle,' he would report during the Greater London Crusade of 1966 to those who were having the service relayed to them in other centres. The information was clearly meant to assist people in the unseen audiences in other parts of the country to make their 'decision', and they were told to go to the front as the crowds were doing in Earl's Court. Similarly, when the Earl's Court Crusade was drawing to its conclusion, Graham in giving 'the invitation', prompted others to respond by using such words as 'tens of thousands will have come to know Christ' – presumably a reference to the thousands who had walked to the front in the preceding weeks. The statistics of those who respond are thus used to buttress the visual argument. The public appeal is *meant* to have an effect on uncommitted onlookers who either observe or hear reports of others going forward.

It is difficult to understand Graham's mind at this point. Although the outward response is represented as 'deciding for Christ', Graham knows that the walk forward does not in itself save anyone. He also knows – as he once indicated in a television interview with Kenneth Harris – that 'to get a small minority of people to really believe' is more biblical than to expect the simultaneous conversion of large crowds. But if the *crowds* are not in fact being converted night by night, as onlookers are led to think, why persist in this invitation method at all? Those who are under the saving operations of the Spirit of God would not suffer from the absence of this method, and they could be put in touch with other Christians without being publicly called forward before the service has ended. One can only conclude, as Pollock has affirmed, that the invitation method is considered to have such an *evangelistic* value that it must be retained. In other words, the action is important, not so much to the individual who comes forward (he may or may

[17]

not later prove spurious), but to the production of the total impression which the common action of a large group makes upon the rest of the meeting – an impression which Graham considers highly desirable.

Doctrinal Implications

As we see it, this brings us to the main point in the present discussion. The convergence of large numbers before the preacher's platform may be very impressive but can it play any part in the conversion of onlookers? Our answer to that depends upon our doctrine of human nature and of the new birth. The issue thus resolves itself into a question which is not simply about evangelistic methods but rather about theological beliefs. What is conversion and how does it take place? What is the work of the Spirit in regeneration, and how does the general work of the Spirit, by which He speaks to the consciences of the unregenerate by the Word, differ from His special and saving work? Did God do no more for Matthew than for other publicans who heard Christ preach and were not converted? Did He do no more for Saul of Tarsus than for other Pharisees who knew the truth and did not respond? Why is it that some believe under the preaching of the gospel and others believe not?

A consideration of these questions will show that the difference between the users and the non-users of 'the invitation' goes much deeper than a question of methodology. Harold J. Ockenga who, as noted earlier, professes to see the difference as only one of methods, himself supplies the evidence to the contrary by the following statement of the belief which underlies the system: 'Some reformed theologians,' he says, 'teach that regeneration by the Holy Spirit precedes conversion. The evangelical position is that regeneration is conditioned upon repentance, confession and faith. This alone stimulates evangelism.'[19] We by-pass the form in which this assertion is made though it is a strange use of the word 'evangelical' to attach it to a view which cannot be found in any of the great evangelical confessions and catechisms of the Reformation and Puritan eras. Ockenga's claim is that man's act must precede the *saving*

[18]

work of the Spirit of regeneration. This is not to say there is no prior activity of the Spirit: 'The Bible makes it plain that the Holy Spirit attends the preaching of the Word and enables a sinner to accept Jesus Christ as Saviour.' The key word is *enables*. The Holy Spirit, according to this view, gives a general help to all who hear the gospel but the final choice rests with the individual; his is the 'decision which results in salvation or reprobation'. Therefore let men be brought to *decision* and their regeneration will follow. Such is the order of salvation according to the invitation system and it is claimed that to teach any other order is to nullify the stimulus for evangelism. Certainly we are prepared to grant that *the whole case for the public appeal can be reduced to the question whether this order of salvation is right or wrong*. If it is wrong 'the invitation' should be given up, which is, of course, an entirely different thing to saying that evangelism should be given up.

Let us turn to see how the belief claimed to be 'the evangelical position' is related to 'the invitation' practice.

When giving 'the invitation' Graham may say, 'You can only come when the Spirit draws you'. By this he evidently means that where a person is willing the Holy Spirit is at work. But what is this *work* which is attributed to the Spirit? It is not regarded as His regenerating work, because at this stage Graham treats men as outside the kingdom until they apply their ability to the decisive act of 'receiving Christ': 'You have that ability to choose, you stand at the crossroads, you may never be as close to the kingdom again, I believe your heart is specially prepared . . . you get up and come forward.'

We waive for the moment this question of a general, enabling work of the Spirit – a work of which both those who are ultimately saved and those who are lost may be the subjects. How does a hearer understand this exhortation of Graham's? The impression he receives is that the willingness he needs is a willingness to come forward, and once the person who has made the public response is seated with his counsellor he is again told that *willingness* is all that is required. Says Charles Riggs: 'When a person is willing to see himself as a sinner and willing to step out by faith to commit his life to Jesus Christ, he

[19]

can do so by simply opening his life to the Saviour. At this point we need to make it very clear and simple. It is like inviting a guest into your house; you invite Jesus Christ to come into your life by faith. In Revelation 3: 20 we have the picture of Jesus Christ standing at the door of the heart, the emotion, intellect and will. He cannot force His way in but will come in where He is invited, and where He is invited He says, "I *will* come in".'

Riggs follows this with the pattern prayer in which the individual 'receives Christ' (already quoted in Graham's own words) and, the decisive step being taken, the counsellor is told: 'It is necessary to show the individual, on the authority of God's Word, what has taken place. Let the enquirer know that *Christ came in* (Rev. 3: 20). Here is a practical question to ask an individual who has just prayed, asking Jesus Christ to come into his heart: "Where is Christ now?" If you have made it simple and the person has understood what he has done, he should be able to say: "He is in my heart." '[20]

All this proceeds on the assumption that if men are brought to a state of willingness, a rubicon has been reached and may at any moment be crossed. Further it is supposed that 'willingness' in an unsaved person is proof that the Spirit has prepared the individual for salvation, because surely the sinner of himself would be unwilling to come to Christ? The argument runs thus:

Major premise: *Only men prepared by the Spirit are willing to receive Christ and be saved.*

Minor premise: *Men willing to receive Christ come forward.*

Conclusion: *Those who come forward to receive Christ are assuredly saved.*

But major and minor premises alike contain a fallacy. The major premise falsely assumes that any willingness which the unregenerate possess is a willingness which is preparatory to conversion and rebirth. The Word of God, however, makes it clear that there may be a temporary willingness and mental consent in the unregenerate which makes them for a time ready to profess Christ while the natural enmity of their hearts towards God is still unremoved (Matt. 13: 20). And such are the windings of the human heart and men's natural blindness in dealing with the concerns of their own souls that it is not necessary to believe this kind of non-saving response only occurs where there is conscious hypocrisy. On the contrary it may be quite sincere. The principle of self-interest in the human heart is sufficient to account for this type of response to the gospel message, especially if such a response has been represented as a means to satisfaction, peace, the solution of besetting problems, and such like.

We may even go further, with Scripture, and say that where the truth is preached there will be a general kind of conviction wrought by the Spirit which disturbs men's consciences and makes them willing to look for some relief. Yet until they have been quickened into newness of life by the special call and operation of the Spirit they will certainly not receive relief in the divinely appointed way, by coming to Christ; rather they will proceed to act on that principle which lies at the root of all natural religion, the belief that *man can do something to put himself right with God*. Thus Herod, with his conscience disturbed by the preaching of John the Baptist, was willing to do 'many things' (Mark 6: 20). This willingness in Herod existed side by side with a basic attitude of hostility towards a holy God. The Scripture never minimizes the fact that the conscience of a natural man may lead him to 'religious' activity while his nature remains unchanged. The peril is that we should imagine such activity to be an initial stage in the process of conversion and to tell people in this condition, as Graham does, that going forward is the 'first step' and that when we take it, God will do the rest. This is appealing to the false principle of works referred to above (which the natural man has always assumed to be true) and it is no wonder if he responds. Nor is it enough to reply that, because people are clearly told they must come forward 'by faith', there can be no danger of a type of salvation by works in the invitation system. Under inadequate gospel preaching, where only man's duty to repent and believe is emphasized and his need of re-birth to *produce* this response is passed over, it is very easy for hearers to confuse their own mental assent with a faith which is not of ourselves but 'the gift of God' (Eph. 2: 8).

Harold J. Ockenga meets the last charge and quotation from Ephesians with a flat denial. He says: 'Faith is erroneously ascribed to God as a gift (see Eph. 2: 8 where "gift" is neuter and "faith" is feminine. Salvation is the antecedent of gift). Man is commanded to repent, to believe, to convert. The Bible places these acts within the ability of man.'[21] This statement brings everything into the open. Faith must not be spoken of as a product of saving grace because it lies within the ability of every man. But much more than a re-translation of Ephesians 2: 8 is needed to prove this. Not a few expositors competent to distinguish between neuter and feminine have held to the correctness of the common translation, and whether, in this particular instance, it is faith which is viewed as the gift of God or the whole salvation, of which faith is a part, the general tenor of the apostle's teaching is plain: faith is 'of the operation of God' (Col. 2: 12); 'unto you it is given in the behalf of Christ . . . to believe on him' (Phil. 1: 29). The real thrust of Ockenga's argument does not depend upon a particular verse but on the assumption that a biblical command implies *ability* on the part of those addressed. This assumption has often been shown to rest upon the fallacious equation of responsibility with ability. Spiritual *inability* is a part of the sin for which man is responsible. For Jesus there was no inconsistency with charging the unbelieving Jews with both responsibility and inability: 'Why do ye not understand my speech? even because ye cannot hear my word. Ye are of your father the devil . . .' (John 8: 43, 44).

What is at stake here is not merely a variation in theological belief. Our charge is that the invitation system leads inevitably to the danger of hastening unregenerate men to confess their 'faith'. In connection with this the words and experience of the late Lewis S. Chafer are noteworthy. Chafer, a well-known American evangelist, himself used the invitation system for some time before he saw reason to abandon the practice. Among the considerations which led him to give up calling hearers to the front he names the following:

'Because of satanic blindness to the Gospel of Grace (2 Cor. 4: 3, 4), unregenerate man cannot comprehend the true basis of salvation, and is therefore ever prone to do the best he knows. This is to attempt to work out his own standing before God by his own efforts. It is this natural tendency to do something of merit that prompts many to respond to the evangelist's appeal . . . A leader with a commanding personality (and every successful evangelist must possess that characteristic in the extreme) may secure the public action of many, when the issue is made one of religious merit through some public act. Under such an impression, a serious person may stand in a meeting who has no conception of what is involved in standing by faith on the Rock Christ Jesus; or he may be persuaded to abandon his natural timidity when he knows nothing of abandoning his satanic tendency to self-help, and resting by faith on that which Christ has done for him. The basis of assurance with all such converts, if questioned carefully, will be found to be no more than a consciousness that they have acted out the programme prescribed for them.'

While it is not necessary for the gospel preacher always to emphasize the truth contained in the Lord's words that men cannot come to Him until specially called by the Father (John 6: 44, 65), it is never permissible to represent an un-regenerate man as being able to do what Scripture declares he will not do (1 Cor. 2: 14; John 5: 40; Rom. 8: 7, etc.). Some may object to this charge on the grounds that Billy Graham, and others who use the invitation method, affirm their belief in human inability apart from the Spirit of God, and in the necessity of the Divine drawing. But it is not here questioned whether Graham accepts the texts which teach this – as a Bible-believer he must do so – the issue concerns the meaning of these terms. The American evangelist believes in a general influence of the Spirit accompanying the Word, which renders men able to respond. But until they do the latter they are still unregenerate: we are 'made alive by trust in Christ'. These are his words, and he confirms this order – first our commitment, *then* our rebirth – in his own testimony: 'they were singing the last verse of the song when I went forward. That first step was the hardest I ever took in my life. But when I took it, God did the rest.'[22] The 'rest' is the new birth. Nowhere does Graham

[23]

teach that it is only when God takes away 'a heart of stone' and implants a new nature that true faith can be exercised. For him, the Holy Spirit provides a general enabling power whereby unregenerate men may fulfil a condition necessary to their rebirth. His evangelistic method accords with this belief. In contrast to this view, we believe that the Scriptures distinguish between a general work of conviction by the Spirit – such as may make an Esau weep and a Felix tremble – and the special, life-conferring call, given by the grace of a sovereign God to those whom He has chosen. Only those who are predestinated receive *this call* and it is clearly stated not to follow justifying faith but to precede it (Rom. 8: 30; Acts 13: 48, etc.) and to *secure* the consent of those to whom it is given (John 6: 36, 37; Eph. 2: 1–8). It is those who are born again who '*see* the kingdom of God' and thus believe the gospel.

We turn to the minor premise in the syllogism:

Men willing to receive Christ come forward.

Certainly if a person who is under the saving operations of the Spirit is told authoritatively by a Christian preacher that he must come forward, he will be likely to do so out of regard for what he believes is God's command. And if such a person is later told that his coming forward was the vital point towards rebirth, he may believe it until he learns better. We are not for a moment asserting that no one is converted where the invitation system is employed, only that the system has, in reality, no *connection* with rebirth. Some are converted in spite of it, and not because of it.

But what of another class of persons, the class who are willing to come to the front and who by this very activity are confused into thinking they are coming to Christ? In their case the premise is false because many unwilling to receive Christ – in the biblical sense of the term – are willing to walk forward. For this large class of persons the theology of the invitation system really leaves no room. It virtually reasons, 'If they are unwilling they would not come forward; if they are willing they must be saved' – an argument which hangs its entire strength on equating 'coming to Christ' with coming to the front, and which supposes that if men have enough will to do the one they can also do the other. The walk forward and the receiving of Christ are both viewed as within the province of human ability, as though there were no essential difference between the ability by which a man goes to the front at a meeting and the power which turns sinners from darkness to light.

Let us also note at this point how the invitation procedure has affected the vocabulary in which the gospel offer is proclaimed to sinners. The words 'believe' and 'repent' are now largely replaced by other terms such as 'Give your life to Christ', 'Open your heart to Christ', 'Do it now','Surrender completely', 'Decide for Christ', etc., and in similar language those who profess conversion are sometimes represented as having 'given in'. To Graham this question of vocabulary is unimportant. Speaking of conversion he says: 'Call it anything you like. Call it dedication. Call it surrender. Call it repentance. Call it grace. Call it anything you like.'[23] But many years ago Professor Albert Dod of Princeton pointed out that the phraseology employed to bring people out in public commitment to Christ during a service *is* significant. Commenting on Charles Finney's favourite phrase, 'submit to Christ' (coupled by Finney with going to the front), Dod observed:

'We are at no loss to understand why Mr. Finney presents the sinner's duty in this form. Submission seems to be more comprised than some other duties within a single mental act, and more capable of instant performance. Were the sinner directed to repent, it might seem to imply that he should take some little time to think of his sins, and of the Being whom he has offended; or if told to believe on the Lord Jesus Christ, he might be led to suppose that he could not exercise this faith until he had called up before his mind the considerations proper to show him his lost condition, and the suitableness of the offered Saviour. Repentance and faith, therefore, will not so well answer his purpose. But with submission, he can move the sinner to the instant performance of the duty involved. . . . In the mental darkness, consequent upon this unscriptural exhibition of his duty, and while flurried and bewildered by the excitement of the scene, the sinner is to perform the double duty of submitting, and of deciding that he has submitted. Who can doubt that, under these circumstances, multitudes have been led to put forth a mental act, and say to themselves, "There, it is done", and then hold up the hand to tell the preacher they have submitted, while their hearts remain as before, except, indeed, that now the mists of religious delusion are gathering over them? Had this system been designed to lead the sinner, in some plausible way, to self-deception, in what important respect could it have been better adapted than it now is to this purpose?'[24]

Conclusions

1. The invitation system, because it represents an outward response as connected with 'receiving Christ', institutes a condition of salvation which Christ never appointed.

2. Because the call to come forward is given as though it were a divine command, those who respond are given reason to believe they are doing something commendable before God, while those who do not are falsely supposed to be disobeying Him.

3. By treating two distinct issues, 'come to Christ' and 'come to the front' as though they were *one*, the tendency of the invitation is to mislead the unconverted in regard to their duty. The real issue is as stated in John 6: 29, 'This is the work of God, that ye believe on him whom he hath sent'. The false is, 'Get up now and come to the front'. 'Thus follows,' says R. L. Dabney, 'unavoidable confusion of conscience. If the person awakened has dignity and good sense, he will probably refuse to come, and then the *drift* of the system is to tell him that *therein* he has rebelled against God and grieved the Holy Ghost; hence, groundless distraction. If he is more gullible, and *goes*, it is implied that he has performed a saving act, or at least one that has *gratia congruens*. It is *in vain they disclaim*; for the common sense reasons, "Why so much urgency, if the means is not truly effective of something?" '[25]

4. A willingness to come to the front on the part of the unconverted may be due to various reasons – natural self-love

[26]

seeking for happiness, a disturbed conscience seeking relief by a religious act, the conditioning influence of a large meeting where others respond, and so on. Because this kind of willingness possible to the unregenerate man cannot, by the very nature of the invitation system, be distinguished from the willingness of those who, by regeneration, have had the natural enmity of their hearts removed, many are led to suppose that their natural willingness (which brings them to the front) is all that is needed to become Christians. The public counselling and prayer which is given them before they leave the meeting serves to confirm them in this idea.

5. Because the invitation system itself precludes the possibility of discrimination between individuals during a public service, the sincere outward response of those who are *still* unconverted is calculated to lead to further unbelief and hardness of heart when they find that no real change has taken place in their lives. 'They feel that a cruel trick has been played upon their inexperience by the ministers and friends of Christianity in thus thrusting them, in the hour of their confusion, into false positions . . . They are conscious that they were thoroughly in earnest in their religious anxieties and resolves at the time, and that they felt strange and profound exercises. Yet bitter and mortifying experience has taught them that *their* new birth and experimental religion at least was a delusion. How natural to conclude that those of all others are delusions also? They say: "The only difference between myself and these earnest Christians is that they have not yet detected the cheat as I have." '[26]

6. There is reason to believe that the number who do go through the form of 'receiving Christ' after an appeal, and who then fall entirely away, is not inconsiderable. 'The thing is so well known,' wrote a last-century observer, 'that in many regions the public coolly expect about forty-five out of fifty, or even a higher ratio, to apostatize ultimately.'[27] In parts of America, where the invitation system has been practised for many years, it has become necessary to record 'second-time decisions', as a number who respond have already done it before. This discredits evangelical truth in the eyes of the world.

[27]

7. Those who do come to a knowledge of Christ through evangelistic services would lose nothing by the omission of 'the invitation', while the hurrying of them into a public act, with its inevitable prominence, may well prove a disservice. Archibald Alexander, one of the founders of the great training school of evangelical preachers at Princeton, New Jersey, who had wide experience of powerful revivals, wrote of the public appeal from his own experience: it 'may bring young people, who are diffident, to a decision, and as it were, constrain them to range themselves on the Lord's side, but the question which sticks with me, is, does this really benefit the persons? In my judgment, not at all, but the contrary. If they have the seed of grace, though it may come forth slowly, yet this principle will find its way to the light and air, and the very slowness of its coming forward, may give it opportunity to strike its roots deep in the earth.'[28]

Similarly R. L. Dabney wrote: 'In almost every case where true grains of living wheat are found among the masses of chaff raked together by these efforts, there will be found a preparatory work in the heart, the result of intelligent scriptural teaching and consistent Christian example, watered for some time by the Holy Spirit in the retirement of their homes. And the only result of the revival appliances as to them has been to hurry them a little, perhaps, in their disclosures of their new feelings, and at the same time to mar and pollute the wholesome soundness of their spiritual character. Had scriptural means of grace been used with them, and no others, they would have come into the church in due time, none the less surely, and with a piety more symmetrical and profound.'[29]

8. The invitation system inevitably directs attention primarily to the outward and the immediately observable, and in so doing serves to support a false standard of judgment. Lewis S. Chafer rightly says: 'Where the spectacular element in public soul-winning is eliminated there is little opportunity to count supposed results, and the test of conversion is taken wholly out of the sphere of profession and made to rest on the reality of a changed life afterwards.'

[28]

9. When the invitation system is employed with apparently great success in crusade meetings, and yet not used in local congregations where ministers can point to no such immediate visible results after services, the impression is effectively conveyed either (i) that the ministry of the churches is not the most effective way of evangelizing or (ii) that the churches should also employ the same programme and methods as are used in crusade meetings. If we accept the first alternative the idea is fostered that 'evangelism' means special meetings with a leader who has a calling distinct from the pastors of congregations. If we accept the second and labour to introduce non-scriptural measures into local churches, there is evidence to show that the long-term effect on consenting congregations is not deeper spirituality and power, but rather the reverse. Evangelism, instead of being a normal part of careful and regular expository preaching, with a twin effect on the consciences of the unconverted and on the growth in grace of Christians, becomes a special, dramatic activity. This leads to an orientation of church life away from Scripture, and as scriptural and non-scriptural duties become confused, the main duties which God requires of Christians and ministers are overshadowed. As Chafer observes: 'The efficiency of the whole company of believers must depend upon their proper adjustment to God in the cleansing and fitting of their individual lives. Just here there is a grave danger lest the church shall ignore her God-appointed work, and the necessary individual preparation for it, and attempt to substitute the wholesale machinery and appeal of the modern evangelist in its place.'[30]

10. The invitation system misconceives the role of an evangelist. The gospel preacher is not a 'spiritual obstetrician' appointed to supervise the new birth of sinners; still less is he called to propose ways which, if complied with, will accomplish the rebirth.

John Kennedy, one of the greatest evangelists of Scotland, whose death in 1884 was described by C. H. Spurgeon as 'a loss to the Highlands greater than could have befallen by the death of any other hundred men', shrewdly saw that the whole tendency of the invitation system, as it was then being first introduced, would be to alter the work of a gospel preacher. According to the new evangelism, he writes:

'Faith is represented as something to be done, in order to salvation; and pains are taken to show that it is an easy thing. Better far than this would it be to see to it, that those with whom they deal are truly convinced of sin, and to labour to set forth Christ before them, in his glorious completeness as a Saviour. To explain faith to them, that they may do it, is to set them still to work, though setting an easier task before them. I know well the tendency there is, at a certain stage of anxious inquiry, to ask, "What is faith, that I may do it?" It is a legalist's work to satisfy that craving; but this is what is done in the "Inquiry-room". "Who is he, that I may believe in him?" was the question asked by one who approached the dawning of a day of salvation. Explanations of what faith is are but trifling with souls. How different is the Scripture way! The great aim there is to "set forth" the object, not to explain the act, of faith. Let there be conviction, illumination and renewal, and faith becomes the instinctive response of the quickened soul to the presentation by God of His Christ; and, without these, no explanation of faith can be helpful to any one. The labour to explain it is too often adapted to the craving of a legal spirit. It were wiser to take pains in removing ignorance and error regarding God, and sin, and Christ. Help them to know these, if you would not build them up with "untempered mortar" in a false peace. If you would be wise, as well as kind, work in that direction, rather than in the hurrying of them to belief.'[31]

'Why is it so that profane and ungodly men think it so easy to believe in Christ? And they say they do it with all their heart, when it's plain by the Scripture they are not such to whom those glorious things of the Gospel do belong.

1. *They think it so easy because they take presumption for faith;* they think they believe because they presume. Now to presume is easy, because it is a work of the flesh; it is suitable to our corruptions. The prophet complained that the Jews, though they committed all lewdness, they would "come and lean themselves upon the Lord" and trust in lying words, saying, "The temple of the Lord", etc. That is not faith which most of the world have; it's presumption, it's carnal confidence, such as those had who said, "Lord, have not we prophesied in thy Name"; such as the foolish virgins had, Matthew 25; and such as Paul had before his conversion when he said, "He was alive", Rom. 7.

2. *They look upon faith in Christ as easy, because they divide the object;* they take some things of Christ not the whole Christ. They think it's only believing on him as a Saviour for pardon of sin; they do not choose him as a Lord to whom in all obedience they resign themselves. This is indeed the rock that splits many, tell them of believing in Christ, and they think that is only to rest on him for salvation, they attend not that it is receiving of Christ for all ends and purposes God sent him into the world. Now one main end besides our justification and salvation is our sanctification: "To redeem to himself a people zealous of good works," Titus 2:14. To communicate his Spirit so as to make holy as well as his merit to make happy. There are many who desire to be the Lord's by redemption but not by sanctification; they would have Christ's blood theirs but not his Spirit . . .

In all Judas' eminency and profession of Christ, he had no true love to Christ, no saving faith. Who can hear of Judas that preaches, that works miracles, that is often in duties with Christ yet he is not sincere? And, therefore, you may observe that our Saviour in all his sermons and parables, did press this

[31]

as the sum of all, to look that we "build upon a Rock", to see that we dig deep in our building, that we be good ground, receiving the seed in a deep and honest heart. No subject did our Saviour so much insist on as this, when yet we would think in those days, when Christ's teaching and miracles were so visible, and outward encouragements to profess him wholly wanting, that none should follow him but upon sincere and upright grounds.'

ANTHONY BURGESS, *Expository Sermons on John 17*, 1656

'It is a pestilent opinion to think that every man may be saved if he do in the general acknowledge Christ. It is said, Acts 2:21 "Whosoever shall call on the name of the Lord shall be saved;" not "on the Lord", but "on the name of the Lord". By the name of the Lord is meant all that which shall be revealed to us of the Lord Jesus in the Scriptures. The meaning is, whosoever doth receive, acknowledge, and worship Christ, according to what the Scriptures do reveal and testify of him, shall be saved. . . . I shall not take upon me to determine what articles are absolutely necessary to salvation; it will be hard to define and we know not by what rule to proceed. In the general, it is exceeding dangerous to lessen the misery of man's nature, the merit and satisfaction of Christ, or the care of good works.'

THOMAS MANTON (1620-1677), *Exposition of John 17*

'I am glad you know when persons are justified. It is a lesson I have not yet learnt. There are so many stony ground hearers, that receive the Word with joy, that I have determined to suspend my judgment till I know the tree by its fruits. . . . The way the Spirit of God takes, is like that we take in preparing the ground: do you think any farmer would have a crop of corn next year unless they plow now; and you may as well expect a crop of corn on unplowed ground, as a crop of grace, until the soul is convinced of its being undone without a Saviour. That is the reason we have so many mushroom converts, so many persons that are always happy! happy! happy! and never were miserable; why? Because their stony ground is not plowed up; they have not got a conviction of the law; they are stony ground hearers; they hear the word with joy, and in a time of temptation, which will soon come after a seeming or real conversion, they fall away. They serve Christ as the young man served the Jews that laid hold of him, who, when he found he was like to be a prisoner for following Christ, left his garments; and so some people leave their profession. That makes me so cautious now, which I was not thirty years ago, of dubbing converts so soon. I love now to wait a little, and see if people bring forth fruit; for there are so many blossoms which March winds you know blow away, that I cannot believe they are converts till I see fruit brought forth. It will do converts no harm to keep them a little back; it will never do a sincere soul any harm.'

GEORGE WHITEFIELD (1714-1770)

'I have sometimes thought when I have heard addresses from some revival brethren who had kept on saying time after time, "Believe, believe, believe," that I should like to have known for myself what it was we were to believe in order to our salvation. There is, I fear, a great deal of vagueness and crudeness about this matter. I have heard it often asserted that if you believe that Jesus Christ died for you, you will be saved. My dear hearer, do not be deluded by such an idea. You may believe that Jesus Christ died for you, and may believe what is not true; you may believe that which will bring you no sort of good whatever. That is not saving faith. The man who has saving faith afterwards attains to the conviction that Christ died for him, but it is not of the essence of saving faith. Do not get that into your head, or it will ruin you. Do not say, "I believe that Jesus Christ died for me," and because of that feel that you are saved. I pray you to remember that the genuine faith that saves the soul has for its main element – trust – absolute rest of the whole soul – on the Lord Jesus Christ to save me, whether he died in particular or in special to save me or not, and relying, as I am, wholly and alone on him, I am saved. Afterwards I come to perceive that I have a special interest in the Saviour's blood; but if I think I have perceived that before

[33]

I have believed in Christ, then I have inverted the Scriptural order of things, and I have taken as a fruit of my faith that which is only to be obtained by rights, by the man who absolutely trusts in Christ, and Christ alone, to save.'

C. H. SPURGEON (1834-1892) *Sermons, vol. 58*, 583-4

'Sometimes we are inclined to think that a very great portion of modern revivalism has been more a curse than a blessing, because it has led thousands to a kind of peace before they have known their misery; restoring the prodigal to the Father's house, and never making him say, "Father, I have sinned." How can he be healed who is not sick? or he be satisfied with the bread of life who is not hungry? The old-fashioned sense of sin is despised, and consequently a religion is run up before the foundations are dug out. Everything in this age is shallow. Deep-sea fishing is almost an extinct business so far as men's souls are concerned. The consequence is that men leap into religion, and then leap out again. Unhumbled they came to the church, unhumbled they remained in it, and unhumbled they go from it.'

C. H. SPURGEON, *The Sword and The Trowel*, 1882

And he said, So is the kingdom of God, as if a man should cast seed into the ground; and should sleep, and rise night and day, and the seed should spring and grow up, he knoweth not how. For the earth bringeth forth fruit of herself; first the blade, then the ear, after that the full corn in the ear. . . .

'Sowers of the seed of eternal life are here implicitly bidden to have faith in the word they preach; for it is the seed of God. When it has found place in a heart, they are not to be tormented with anxiety concerning the final issue, as though they were to keep it alive, and that it could only live through them; for this of maintaining its life is God's part and not theirs, and He undertakes to fulfil it (1 Pet. 1: 23-25). They are instructed also to rest satisfied that it should grow and spring up without their knowing the exact steps of this growth. Let them not be searching at its roots to see how they have stricken into the soil, nor seek prematurely to anticipate

[34]

the shooting of the blade, or the forming of the corn in the ear; for the mystery of the life of God in any and in every heart is unsearchable; all attempts to determine that its course shall be exactly this way, or that way, can only work mischief. It has a law, indeed, of orderly development, *"first the blade, then the ear, then the full corn in the ear"*; words which suggest a comparison with 1 John 2: 12–14, where in like manner the Apostle distributes the faithful, according to their progress in the spiritual life, into "little children", "young men", and "fathers"; but this law is hidden; and the works of God in nature, where He never *exactly* repeats Himself, are not more manifold than are his works in grace. Therefore let the messengers of the Gospel be content that the divine word should grow in a mysterious manner, and one whereof the processes are hidden from themselves; and, the seed once sown and having taken root, let them commit what remains to God, being satisfied that this seed is incorruptible, and that He will bring his own work to perfection.'

RICHARD TRENCH on 'The Seed Growing Secretly' in his
Notes on The Parables of our Lord

'American Protestantism is characterized by a peculiar evil which I may describe by the term "spurious revivalism." It has been often called the "New Measure System." The common mischief resulting from all its forms is the over-hasty reception into the communion of the churches, of multitudes of persons whom time proves to have experienced no spiritual change. This disastrous result is in some churches wrought without the machinery of sensational excitements as where Pelagian or ritualistic teachings encourage men to come in heedlessly and coldly upon a mere profession of historical faith. In most cases, however, these mischievous accessions are brought about by sensational human expedients. The ill-starred artists stimulate natural remorse and the merely sympathetic excitements of the natural feelings and deceive themselves and encourage their victims to be deceived into mistaking these agitations for the real and saving work of the Holy Spirit with a criminal recklessness. They overlook the vital distinctions which the religious guide ought to make, which I have pointed out in the twenty-first article of my *Collected Discussions* volume 1, in exposition of 1 Corinthians 3 : 10-15.

This lamentable art has grown in America to great dimensions; the victims of its deception are to be counted by myriads. Its effects for good are so evanescent, that a religious profession has become contemptible in the eyes of critical worldly men. Many churches are loaded down with dead members. Church discipline becomes impracticable. This nominal membership includes tens of thousands of silent infidels who have inferred from the manifest deceitfulness of their own hot religious experience the deceptiveness of the gospel itself. The average standard of Christian morals is degraded throughout the country. The experience of a long life compels me sorrowfully to testify against this method of accessions as the grand peril and curse of American Protestantism. It has shorn the gospel among us of the larger part of its purifying power, and Christ of his honour, until our average Protestantism can scarcely boast of higher moral results than American popery. The mortifying result is, that after ninety years of boasted activity and asserted success in this species of evangelism in these United States, breeding and good manners, domestic purity, temperance, business morals and political morals, are at a lower ebb than in any nation in Protestant Christendom. The evil has become gigantic, and demands solemn protest and resistance.

I know it is an unpopular thing for a minister of the gospel to bear this witness. But it is true. And my regard for that account which I must soon render at a more awful bar than that of arrogant public opinion demands its utterance.'

R. L. DABNEY, *Discussions*, vol. 3, 1892, 563-4

'Most would agree with my sixth point which is that this method tends to produce a superficial conviction of sin, if any at all. People often respond because they have the impression that by doing so they will receive certain benefits. I remember hearing of a man who was regarded as one of the "star converts" of a campaign. He was interviewed and asked why he had gone forward in the campaign the previous year. His answer was that the evangelist had said, "If you do not want to 'miss the boat' you had better come forward." He said that he did not want to "miss the boat" so he had gone forward; and all the interviewer could get out of him was that he somehow felt that he was now "on the boat". He was not clear about what this meant, not what it was, and nothing had seemed to happen to him during the subsequent year. But there it was; it can be as superficial as that.

Or take another illustration out of my own experience. In the church where I ministered in South Wales I used to stand at the main door of the church at the close of the service on Sunday night, and shake hands with people as they went out. The incident to which I am referring concerns a man who used to come to our service every Sunday night. He was a tradesman but also a heavy drinker. He got drunk regularly every Saturday night, but he was also regularly seated in the gallery of our church every Sunday night. On the particular night to which I am referring I happened to notice while preaching that this man was obviously being affected. I could see that he was weeping copiously, and I was anxious to know what was happening to him. At the end of the service I went and stood at the door. After a while I saw this man coming, and immediately I was in a real mental conflict. Should I, in view of what I had seen, say a word to him and ask him to make his decision that night, or should I not? Would I be interfering with the work of the Spirit if I did so? Hurriedly I decided that I would not ask him to stay behind, so I just greeted him as usual and he went out. His face revealed that he had been crying copiously, and he could scarcely look at me. The following evening I was walking to the prayer-meeting in the church, and, going over a railway bridge, I saw this same man coming to meet me. He came across the road to me and said, "You know, doctor, if you had asked me to stay behind last night I would have done so." "Well," I said, "I am asking you now, come with me now." "Oh no," he replied, "but if you had asked me last night I would have done so." "My dear friend," I said, "if what happened to you last night does not last for twenty-four hours I am not interested in it. If you are not as ready to come with me now as you were last night you have not got the right, the true thing. Whatever affected you last night was only temporary and passing, you still do not see your real need of Christ."

That is the kind of thing that may happen even when an appeal is not made. But when an appeal is made it is greatly exaggerated and so you get spurious conversions. As I have reminded you even John Wesley, the great Arminian, did not make appeals to people to "come forward". What you find so often in his Journals is something like this: "Preached at such and such a place. Many seemed to be deeply affected, but God alone knows how deeply." Surely that is very significant and important. He had spiritual understanding and knew that many factors can affect us. What he was concerned about was not immediate visible results but the work of the Holy Spirit in regeneration. A knowledge of the human heart, of psychology, should teach us to avoid anything that increases the possibility of spurious results.'

D. M. LLOYD-JONES, (giving eight
reasons against 'Calling for Decisions',
Preaching and Preachers, 1971, 275-76)

References

1 Leighton Ford, *The Christian Persuader* (New York, 1966), 138.

2 These were Graham's words at Earl's Court on June 27, 1966. Unless otherwise indicated, future quotations are given from other words he spoke during the crusade meetings.

3 Curtis Mitchell, *Those Who Came Forward* (The World's Work Ltd. 1966), 32.

4 Mitchell, 33.

5 John Pollock, *Billy Graham* (London, 1966), 235.

6 Mitchell, 42–43.

7 Pollock, 184.

8 Albert Dod, *Essays, Theological and Miscellaneous* (1847), 126.

9 *Study Papers of World Congress on Evangelism*, 26 Oct.–4 Nov., 1966.

10 *The Christian*, July 8, 1966, 24.

11 William James (1842–1910), American philosopher and psychologist.

12 Ford, 124.

13 An article 'How Does Graham Do It?' in *New Christian*, June 2, 1966.

14 Mitchell, 22.

15 It may be observed that while Graham says 'There's nothing about the mechanics of coming forward that saves anybody's soul' (Pollock, 306), too many statements of this kind suggest the contrary to the average person.

16 Mitchell, 37.

17 Quoted by Austin Phelps, *The Theory of Preaching* (New York, 1882), 286.

18 Mitchell, 40.

19 *Study Papers*.

20 Life and Witness Classes, Lecture 4, printed in *The Christian*, June, 1966.

21 *Study Papers*.

22 Mitchell, 33.

23 Mitchell, 22.

24 *Essays, Theological and Miscellaneous*, 128–9.

25 R. L. Dabney, *Discussions* (Reprint 1967), vol. 1, 568.

26 Dabney, 572.

27 Dabney, 566.

28 Archibald Alexander, *Thoughts on Religious Experience* (Reprint 1967), 72.

29 Dabney, 571.

30 Lewis S. Chafer, *True Evangelism* (1911), 19.

31 John Kennedy, *A Reply to Dr. Bonar's Defence of Hyper-Evangelism* (Edinburgh, 1875), 30. For a defence of the practice which Kennedy opposed see R. A. Torrey's *How to Work for Christ*, Bk. II, Chap. 14, 'The After Meeting'. Outside those areas where the old evangelism has held its ground, Torrey's book with its sub-title, 'A Compendium of Effective Methods' has been widely followed since its first publication in 1901.

Other titles by Iain H. Murray

REVIVAL AND REVIVALISM
The Making and Marring of American Evangelicalism 1750-1858

'Anyone interested in revivals of religion, whether that interest grows primarily out of the academy or the church, will find *Revival and Revivalism* a valuable new resource.

PROFESSOR GARTH M. ROSEN,
GORDON-CONWELL THEOLOGICAL SEMINARY.

'In the hands of a researcher such as Iain Murray, history is an encouraging breath of fresh air, with practical lessons for us today.'

ROSS PULLIAM,
EDITOR OF *THE INDIANAPOLIS NEWS*.

ISBN 0 85151 660 2
480pp. Cloth-bound. Illustrated.

PENTECOST-TODAY?
The Biblical Basis and Understanding of Revival

Iain Murray has already approached the subject of revival from several historical angles. Now he confronts the biblical teaching and presents what the Bible has to say about this all-important, much-debated matter.

ISBN 0 85151 747 1
Approx. 300p. Cloth-bound.

SPURGEON v. HYPER-CALVINISM
The Battle for Gospel Preaching

Fellow Baptists of Hyper-Calvinism persuasion condemned Spurgeon for believing that Calvinistic orthodoxy could be held along with 'impassioned appeal to every sinner to come to Christ and be saved'. Iain Murray elaborates the issues involved.

ISBN 0 85151 692 0
184pp. Paperback.

D. MARTYN LLOYD-JONES

The First Forty Years, 1899-1939
Volume 1 of the Authorised Biography

'The events that transported Martyn Lloyd-Jones from a glamorous Harley Street medical practice to a pastorate in an impoverished Welsh mining town make a magnificent biography.'

CHRISTIANITY TODAY

ISBN 0 85151 353 0
412pp. Cloth-bound. Illustrated.

D. MARTYNLLOYD-JONES

The Fight of Faith, 1939-1981
Volume 2 of the Authorised Biography

The ministry of Martyn Lloyd-Jones at Westminster Chapel which began at the outbreak of World War II was suddenly changed at the point in which this volume begins. His hard work in the difficult War and post-War years became the preparation for his great influence in London in the fifties and sixties. But theses pages trace his ministry into wider circles - to the Universities, to Europe, the United States, South Africa and ultimately, in his books, to the whole world.

ISBN 0 85151 564 9
826pp. Cloth-bound. Illustrated.

AUSTRALIAN CHRISTIAN LIFE FROM 1788

Australian Christian Life is an introduction to a remarkable period of history. Nominally 'Christian', the early colony was largely licentious, brutal and pagan; the least likely of all places to be a successful mission field.

But Christian history is a history of surprises. from such unpromising beginnings an heroic form of resolute Christianity began to make its way among soldiers, convicts, merchants and, at long last, Aborigines also.

ISBN 0 85151 524 X
384pp. Cloth-bound. Illustrated.

JONATHAN EDWARDS
A New Biography

Edwards' theology is set here in its proper context of his everyday life. We are able to follow him in public and private - as pastor in the days of the Great Awakening as well as in the 'wilderness' years in the outpost Stockbridge. This outstanding study of a great man of God serves as a classic illustration of how the church today can and should learn from its past history.

ISBN 0 85151 704 8
536pp. Large paperback. Illustrated.

THE FORGOTTEN SPURGEON

An incisive, historical and theological insight into the great 19th century Baptist, with emphasis on the doctrines that moulded his life and thought.

ISBN 0 85151 156 2
256pp. Paperback.

For free illustrated catalogue please write to:
THE BANNER OF TRUTH TRUST
3 Murrayfield Road, Edinburgh EH12 6EL
P.O. Box 621, Carlisle, Pennsylvania 17013, U.S.A.